# HEALING
# WORDS

# HEALING
# WORDS

**A Collection of Verse
to Aid in Healing
from an Unhealthy
and Abusive Childhood**

**Janet Osmond**

**BALBOA.**
PRESS
A DIVISION OF HAY HOUSE

Balboa Press books may be ordered through booksellers or by contacting:

Balboa Press
A Division of Hay House
1663 Liberty Drive
Bloomington, IN 47403
www.balboapress.com
1-(877) 407-4847

Cover Image: Painting by Janet Osmond

ISBN: 978-1-4525-7591-9 (sc)
ISBN: 978-1-4525-7592-6 (e)

Library of Congress Control Number: 2013910358

Printed in the United States of America.

Balboa Press rev. date: 06/21/2013

*For my amazing Counsellor, precious Daughter,*
*incredible Husband and the one and only Louise Hay—*
*these four people saved my life.*

*With eternal love and gratitude to you all.*

# PREFACE

I didn't actually decide to write this book!

One day I wrote a poem—I read the poem to my husband and daughter and they liked it—a writer was born? It was in December 2012 and we were all busy with Christmas preparations, so I made a mental note that once January dawned, I would start to write some more poems.

I began writing poetry—my kind of poetry—as a form of writing out my pain. I have done much personal development work during the last 3 years but still felt that I was holding onto an inordinate amount of pain. Maybe I could 'write it out' was something that I'd thought and that was the beginning of my writing.

I found as I wrote each poem that emotions would arise so instead of writing only the 'darkest' words, I created some happy rhymes too to intersperse between the more serious offerings. I had told my friends what I was doing and of course, they asked to hear what I had written. When I read one or two poems to them, it became clear to us both that the content was interchangeable from my life into their own—maybe some details were different—but my words resonated with them.

Suddenly I knew—I had always harboured an urge, throughout the whole of my life, to be able to help other people. This would be my medicine which I could offer up to the world and if I can help just ONE PERSON to deal with the hell in their own life, I will feel jubilation beyond compare.

So I've scribbled away with my pen (somehow it felt right to do it this way) then transferred them to my computer and we decided to collate them into a book . . . here is my book. I hope sincerely that you can find some comfort, some understanding or just a place to feel safe.

I offer these poems from my heart to yours—enjoy.

With my love

Janet Osmond

# INTRODUCTION

This book of poetry covers my own personal journey into healing from an unhealthy and unhappy childhood—a journey that many of you will recognise—I am sure.

The writing has proven to be cathartic and I have transcribed it into book form, in the hope that what I have experienced may be of help or comfort to others.

I also hope very strongly, that it will help others not to feel so ALONE. That was my underlying feeling throughout the whole of my life until around 3 years ago. By explaining how I have felt, maybe someone can feel supported sufficiently to carry on battling through, for I do believe that everything happens for a reason and that everything I need to know will be revealed to me—at exactly the right time.

It is so easy to feel that you are the only person who has felt a certain way or has had certain experiences and to realise that someone else understood how and what I was feeling was very helpful to me.

This then is the aim of my book of poems—to convey my understanding and offer my love to you to help with your own journey.

With love

Janet Osmond

# CONTENTS

# EMOTIONS

I've started writing poetry—and I am so surprised!
I haven't been poetic, at any time in my life
I started to write what was in my head, a story to be told
But as I wrote I found, that emotions began to unfold

At first their content was quite dark, with serious issues inside
But soon amusing subjects arose, with which I identified
Whenever I would start to write, it was always a surprise
To find what would come up for me, that I could verbalise

Soon it was clear that with the words, emotions were entwined
And as I wrote I could release them, from my body and my mind
How are emotions held inside, I wonder where they're stored
I do know this: that once invoked, they cannot be ignored

Very powerful experiences, hold emotions of equal depth
As they rise into my consciousness, my body begins to stress
I feel anxious in my stomach, unsure and ill at ease
Emotions giving notice, that they can create dis-ease

So honour your emotions, grant them time to spend with you
Give their message recognition—learn what you need to do
Treated in this special way, their purpose identified
Will allow emotions to dissipate, and not be stored inside

So I'll continue choosing subjects—actually, they make themselves known
And as I lay the words down, seeds of healing have been sown
It seems I've found a therapy—inside my poetry
I will continue writing—hoping it helps you as well as me

# DISCOVERY

Your mind can find things, that have hurt you before
Though you've pushed them away, and closed the door
A week or a month, or a lifetime ago
It's all still there, whether you want to know

So the question I'd ask, is who runs my mind
When it keeps all the things, I chose to leave behind
My clever mind, concealed the worst of my pain
Until it decided, I'd managed to remain sane

I was driving home from work, with the radio on
Listening to a lady, revealing what went wrong
In her life it was—though it sounded like mine
I listened intently, as I discovered his crime

When my mind decided to take me within
To give me the details of my stepfather's sin
I was not prepared for what I would find
All the images and flashbacks and hurt in my mind

I was 43 years old, before my mind would unfold
And tell me exactly, what had never been told
So difficult to realise, it had all been so wrong
As a child you just accept, whatever is going on

## DISCOVERY Continued

But the child that I'd been, had now started to scream
I was beginning to wish, it was all a bad dream
My head was spinning, and I couldn't see straight
As my mind illustrated, what had been my fate

I was frightened as well—who on earth could I tell?
Would my husband still love me?—I felt suddenly unwell
Burning anger raged inside, hot tears on my cheeks
But what to do I did not know, I felt like such a freak

'Sexual Abuse' it had a name, that's why it had felt so bad
It's not supposed to happen, between a Daughter and her Dad
The reason I'd tried to end my life—it had ALL been his fault
Instantly—I hated him—it hit me with a jolt

I'd end up in a children's home, was the threat held over me
If I ever told what was happening—I retreated internally
I'd lived my whole life long in fear—how could I deal with this
But to give up now I'd found the truth, well that would be remiss

I found it so disturbing, how ingrained my anger was
As I started to unlock the doors, and calculate my loss
Anger proved to be the fuel, forcing me to ask for help
So my icy block of emotion, could finally start to melt

## SNOW

Brilliant white and pristinely pure, is how I see the snow
Soft and enveloping, and blanketing the ground below
In moonlight all is bright and clear—a gentle peaceful light
Whilst sunshine makes it sparkle and shine—a fairy story sight

Each snowflake is amazing, so beautiful and new
Fantastic shapes—not one the same—so white they're almost blue
Perfection grows in crystal form, each tiny piece of art
Created by the universe, of which we're all a part

Magnificent formations, on mountains, fields and trees
Softening forms and angles, rippling like the seas
No one thing stands out from the rest—so easy on the eye
It's like a huge marshmallow, has descended from the sky

Each snowstorm ends in silence, and a stillness so serene
For me it's one of nature's gifts—a deeply enjoyable scene
Snow holds a fascination, that has never gone away
So snow upon the hillside, gives me a perfect day

# REALISATION

Once the awful realisation, of what I'd lived through, had sunk in
I considered who I could talk to, about such a disturbing thing
It couldn't be my husband, I was terrified he'd be repulsed
And if he couldn't stay with me, my sanity would be engulfed

I trembled at the idea of that, thoughts threatening to explode
Inside my head, as the details of my story were being told
It was pouring out in pictures, from the film reels in my head
I felt quite sick and dizzy—I truly wished that I was dead

I considered all my friends and came up with a total blank
No-one could be prepared, for the things in my memory bank
Another family member—brother, sister or my mum
I didn't dare involve them, now I felt frightened as well as numb

I struggled to eat and to sleep, there was no escape to be found
From the flashbacks in my memory, spinning round and round
Staring with unseeing eyes, as all the images played out
I was the unwilling audience, realising what my life was about

Hard to convey how much it hurt, when as the images appeared
The truly harrowing feelings, created screaming in my ears
It wasn't that I'd been screaming—all those years ago
But rather my soul shouting loud: 'you just had to know'

# WHO ARE WE?

Who are you and who am I . . .
People who came from the sky
Our bodies made from stars and such
Galaxy-making magic dust

With minds as wide and deep as night
Full of wisdom—that's out of sight . . .
How to reach our potential, we say
Maybe promise to 'just be' every day

To sit in silence with ears open wide
May allow some real knowledge, to slip deep inside
Informing, advising and guiding our lives
A powerful force joins us to the skies

Universal one—all part of the whole
Supporting and caring, for each of our souls
When all is re-learned, we'll return to the one
And then we will know, that our work is all done

# COMPLEX PEOPLE

There are lots of complex people, living complicated lives
Who don't realise that their problems, are created in their minds
And people's lives though different, are strangely all the same
For everyone is trying hard, to make themselves feel sane

Complex conversations—played out solely in our heads
Most will never have a voice, so will just remain unsaid
The same old conversation, can be re-run over again
With subtle little changes, that sound better in our brain

Complex problem-solving—of a problem which doesn't exist
Can take up many hours, as each solution is dismissed
'Just being well prepared' or 'Thinking things through'
Is how we describe this process—but it's painfully untrue

Complex self-destruction—a mental programme we all use
Prevents us knowing our true selves, so ego cannot lose
Our destructive self-talk, convinces us we are badly flawed
And that everyone who meets us, recognises us as a fraud

Complex imagination, creates inner worlds only we can know
Where we live alone in fear, of letting any of it show
We hide our strange beliefs, which shape and mould our little lives
I pray this veil of fiction, will one day be dissolved, from our minds

# DROWNING

There isn't enough help around, once the lock's been sprung
Black memories and images, from when you were very young
It's shocking to re-live those times, and hard to fight on through
Transported back to unkind days—when the hurt person is you

Pain oozes from the crevices, in arms, and hands, and feet
It's stored in every part of you—in every piece of meat . . .
And bone and hair and tendon—nowhere is sacrosanct
In fact it felt like I was just, one great big ball of angst

Emotions feel like poison, surging strong, and straight, and true
They are the message keepers, of the things that happen to you
There is no escape from feelings, they stay with you all your days
Until you turn and face them—allowing them to drain away

So often it's mental overload—too much information sent
Too hard for me to work through, I beg my mind to relent
Keep sieving through the wreckage, of the little girl I was
Those precious years have gone now—that feels like such a loss

## DROWNING Continued

It's those things that are hardest—such as innocence all gone
Never to come back again and I'm not sure how to move on
I wondered what it would be like, to feel pure and good inside
I couldn't know, all I had felt was the need for me to hide

You do begin to wonder—are there enough pieces left?
To put myself back together—or will I always feel bereft
Did the key and important parts, of the essence that is me
Withstand the cruel behaviour, that I had lived to see

The answer is a resounding YES—the essence of me was safe
It curled up tight and small, and hid itself in a special place
Now it is unfurling—beautiful, pure and good
I am so excited to meet me, as I spring out from my bud

## HELP

I'm writing all this poetry, in the hope that it helps you
Then when you're feeling better, you'll pass it on to one or two
Maybe to your partner—or your children sat at home
Your parents or your colleagues—they're all struggling alone

We sense that we're unhappy, though we don't understand why
We choose from the selection, of problems we see in our life
Your partner didn't help you, or your child just answered back
Doesn't matter who you blame—they're only taking the flack

Therefore if you can be honest—with yourself at least
You'll admit it has been many years, since you've felt real peace
Dissatisfied throughout your life—it's the same for all of us
You know it well, so please decide—you've finally had enough

We already have all the information, that's necessary for our care
It might be hard to look inside—but know that the answer's there
Then summon up your courage, to face your hidden fears
It's the only way to ease your pain and gradually dry your tears

# MUSIC

Music has such meaning, different for all of us
A certain song can lift your mood and really cheer you up
But in just the same manner, a tune will come along
And the memories that it invokes, are sad as well as strong

Sometimes it is the lyrics, that bring a tear into my eye
And then again it may just be, a tune that makes me cry
A song that holds a special place, from a very happy time
Or one played at the funeral, of a precious friend of mine

A song sung by a child, it seems can always hold my ear
Just as a song on karaoke—always gets a cheer
Then there's Christmas Carols, people singing at the door
But better still inside the church, it's stronger than before

Hymns for a funeral, are chosen with great care
Or a wedding celebration, when everyone is there
Voices raised together, create a glorious sound
That I still find more special, than anything else I've found

## SILENCE OF A CHILD

Silent mouth—silent mind
Sounds wrapped up and buried inside
Keeping quiet, to stay sane
Even though, it happened again

Pain and worry, hurt and fear
Can't my mother see what's happening here?
Did I hide it so well, that she could not tell . . .
Or was her sacrifice—my life?

For she was my idol, my princess, my life
But despite all of that, she was simply his wife
The child or the man—my life in her hands
My mother, my jailer, my nothing—I am

I am still here, and have now faced the fear
Being true to myself, I do not keep her near
Forgiveness for her, equals peace just for me
Caring for her at a distance, for now I can be

Her pain and her misery were evident to see
Just not to a child—and that child was me

# UNSEEN

There is no point—I heard him say—the man in front of me
No point in asking anyone, when they just don't want to see
What's there, is in view of everyone—if they would just look
They'd see the cruel and awful things—but they don't give a f—k

No-one wants to look, if they might see something that's wrong
Don't want to be the one to say, that something bad is going on
They'd rather feign ignorance, and pretend that they don't know
So the victim keeps the crime hidden, and doesn't let it show

How can we ever change this, I hope I'd want to help someone
I knew was being victimised or brazenly stood on
I hope and pray that I would be, the one to shout out loud
If a person that I came across, wasn't able to make a sound

I don't suppose we ever know, until the day we're called to arms
So I've gathered up my courage and I'll summon all my charms
I am determined to make a difference, when the spotlight lands on me
The universe demands it, I'll do my best—I guarantee

## ABUSE

My mother remarried and life changed for me
Here is my account, of exactly how it was to be
Just a 2 year old girl, taken to be a man's daughter
In reality a lamb, being led to the slaughter

How could he see anything sexual in that
I do not understand his psychological lack
A strange and infected life he must have led
To nurture such thoughts, inside his head

I wonder how on earth, he first approached me
Perhaps as I sat, on my new Daddy's knee?
What the hell did he say, or do that first day?
My mind has been kind, and washed that away

Many years later—forty-one actually
I found strength inside, to find some therapy
My Counsellor explained, that it was not about sex
It was about control—he was a self-doubting wreck

## ABUSE Continued

I must state at last, some words for his case
For the rest of the time, he was not a disgrace
He looked after my health, and gave me a home
He fed me and clothed me, until I was grown

At home only he, showed any kindness to me
So without him, I didn't know where I would be
He was not cruel, like my step brother and mother
So in my mind, he was way up above her

So difficult now, to explain how things were
But I just had no love or connection to her
As a child, things are . . . just the way that things are
It's only when you have grown, you discover the scars

I hope now he knows, that it was so wrong
And has some idea, of the damage he's done
I've forgiven him now—to set myself free
And despite everything, now I'm glad I am me

## SUNRISE

From the night time so dark, feeling quite crisp and cold
Each morning, brings a magical sight to behold
Sometimes it's quite subtle, and sometimes so bold
The sunrise was created to speak to our soul

Sunrise is the start, to each of our days
As it chases the darkness of night time away
Golden or red and all the shades in-between
Colour spreading outward—a sight so serene

Purple and orange, pink and yellow
The whole sky lit up, with a beautiful glow
Do you wish—as I do, we could freeze-frame the skies
When their beauty takes hold of our hearts through our eyes

# FEELINGS

Aren't Feelings just the oddest things, that we're never taught to use
When actually emotions provide us, with some very important clues
If we acknowledge an emotion—and the feeling that's attached
It will help us to become aware, of exactly what we will attract

What we send out into this universe, is what we will get back
So if we don't enjoy our lives, we've obviously lost the knack
Of creating our own future, exactly how we'd want it to be
Understanding we all have the option, to live with a will that is free

Each morning we can make a decision, on how our day will unfold
Are you aware it is your choice—or did this secret remain untold?
Simply decide within your mind, that you will enjoy the coming day
Then no-one else can influence, the way your emotions will play

Whatever events should come about, or whatever others may do
You've decided to see the positive side, no negative vibes for you
Choose also not to judge anyone, as you enjoy this brand new day
Then negative thoughts can't sneak in, you'll keep them all at bay

It can really be this simple—to create happiness in your own life
Much more healthy and pleasant, than filling your time with strife
As you find the courage inside, to become master of your thoughts
Your mind will unleash it's magic—and you can begin to be taught

# JOURNEY FROM CHILDHOOD

Making a mess, or always being in the way
Seemed to be my only reasons, for living each day
No talking, interaction, laughter or fun
Just 'do this' or 'do that', until the day was done

Eat what you're given, no talking at tea
Food quite inedible, given to me
Sit there till you eat it—you'll sit there all night
Why did most mealtimes, have to end in a fight?

My will against theirs—and they always won
No matter the subject, their will would be done
At first I'd try to explain, just how I felt
How unfair and unjustly, my cards had been dealt

My voice went unheard, 'till I hardly spoke at all
When all else failed, I would talk to the wall
So, lonely and silent another day spent
Trying to fathom out, what it all meant

Why did they each, dislike me so much
My family, schoolfriends, neighbours and such
It must just be me—they could all see—I was not fit to be
And I knew God in heaven, was also looking down on me

So . . . God knew I was bad, that must be why I had . . .
Such a horrid existence—the whole world was mad
Just endure what I had, and hope for a time
When I could escape, from this prison of mine

## JOURNEY FROM CHILDHOOD Continued

Now as I look back, fifty years have gone by
The pain and the fear, are still in my minds' eye
Emotions within, where that fear still hides
Sends turmoil coursing, in huge raging tides

Amazing to find, the power of my own mind
Which will help me escape, from the bonds that bind
Erasing all negative memories, from my head
Positive emotions, are taking over, instead

My family were all suffering, in their own ways
Throughout their lives—and I fear, on to their graves
For myself, thank goodness, I've now seen the light
And can cherish my memories, with love and insight

I am now strong, and have learned many things
From my old memories, and the wisdom they bring
Having studied and read, I now feel so alive
I have challenged the things, that were stored deep inside

Spring cleaning the rooms, inside my own mind
I am choosing to leave, all that madness behind
Cleared out my prison, and all of it's chains
At last I can state, that 'Positivity Reigns'!

# CHANGE

Change is very often seen, as an extremely unwelcome state
Though the whole universe employs change, in order to create
'A change is better than a rest'—or so the saying goes
What it actually means is, it'll keep you on your toes

Change is healthy for us, and it helps to develop our minds
Doing different and new things, stops us from falling behind
Having new places to go, and new decisions for us to make
Can put excitement in our life, and help us to create

Change is the opposite of stagnation, and being in a rut
But it gives most people I know, a strange feeling in their gut
It's such a scary sensation, that our reactions are intense
Making us always answer 'no'—which can often cause offence

Change can be exciting, something new to think about
But we're usually too frightened, to feel anything but doubt
If offers something new to learn, or new options we can try
Still we can't escape the fear, so we decide not to comply

Change is such a massive word, when it's applied in our own life
We want to run and hide from it—it cuts us like a knife
It's just a threat to all we know, and we're not brave enough to try
So even when we say we will—it's usually a lie

Consider the way you feel toward change—decide to feel it's good
So every time it shows it's face, you can welcome it with love
The first time you embrace change—and find happiness inside
You will have found the answer, and never again need to hide

# TIME

Time is a part of all our lives, from the moment we are born
It measures out the way we live, and begins each day at dawn
Seconds add up to minutes, then into hours these will turn
Just 24 such hours—provides a whole day from which to learn

It's used to guide all of our days, at school or work or play
We seem to have inbuilt timetables, planning out each day
Time to get up, time to eat—parents giving kids a knock
No activity is exempt—we're all governed by the clock

Timing is important—for some key parts of our lives
We have to choose a date and time, when as babies we arrive
Birthdays are all recorded, precious memories we align
Death is our final appointment—and we cannot choose the time

## THE WILDERNESS YEARS

Once the bomb had landed and exploded in my mind
It took some time to realise, how much strength I'd have to find
I understood: it was not my fault—and finally I could see
That he had been the adult, and the innocent child was me

Though that was the most important point—to know I wasn't 'bad'
It couldn't wipe away, all the pain and suffering I'd had
I seemed to drown initially, in the soup of hurt I'd found
That heightened all my senses—as it became unbound

It transpired every day, there was something new to know
Emotions causing havoc—now released from down below
A whirlwind sleeping inside me, had now started to spin
It picked me up and hurled me around—I thought that it might win

This battle raging deep inside, to find my true good self
For so long I'd felt I wasn't fit to live, as I was beyond help
Days and weeks, months flew by—I don't know where they went
I'd drag myself on through each day, and in the morning wake up spent

A year had gone and then a few more, how I wished I wasn't here
Why had my mind started this—when my journey wasn't clear
I floundered in such sadness, that permeated to my soul
I could not make any sense of it—what on earth could be my goal

## THE WILDERNESS YEARS Continued

It didn't seem that I could survive, the poisons contained in me
All I could think, was that I really wasn't meant to be
Perhaps that was my true life path, a suicide, a sacrifice
I went through hell and back again, but clung on to my life

In all it took ten years, of trying to understand myself
Never feeling certain and wishing I was somebody else
I existed in a twilight world—everything dark—nothing clear
Wondering if I could hold on to, those people I held dear

Luckily I met another lady—found a book, and my life began
It was time for me to rebuild myself, from the crumbs left by that man
I really haven't had time to look back, and reflect on where I've been
It's all happened so quickly—with healing in every scene

So if YOU are in your Wilderness Years, then remind yourself of me
I am so proud that I clung on—we are all meant to be
And now I hope to help you . . . and you . . . . and you . . . and you
Because YOU're so important and your bliss is overdue

# ALONE

Why did I feel so alone—like I was existing in a bubble
I knew if I talked about my life, I'd be in serious trouble
So I isolated myself away, from everyone that I knew
I wouldn't drop my guard or put my troubles on view

I came across as unfriendly, even snooty or aloof
But these labels I preferred, to the one that was the truth
If anyone knew what was going on, inside my little life
They'd use that knowledge against me—another cruel slice

Quiet was my demeanour and it had to stay that way
For even as I grew up, I knew I must continue to allay
Things that screamed and shouted, inside my head at night
All I really knew for sure, was they definitely weren't right

This made for a very lonely life, keeping everyone at arm's length
Not knowing how to cope with it, feeling I hadn't got the strength
Blundering on at the edge of life, when I ought to have been inside
It was such a sad and lonely place to be, this must be emphasised

## ALONE Continued

If you are someone who felt as I did, until halfway through my life
Take comfort that it can all change, once you find your guiding light
For me it was my self-help books, they got me on the path
Now I am bent on helping you and working out the math

If I can help just two people—and they can each, help two more
It won't take us very long, to make the world happier than before
It isn't a great science, that we're trying to employ
Just linking in to common sense, will help us all enjoy

The lives that we were sent to live, on this beautiful planet earth
Now you and I can become a part, of the good in the universe
And working together as part of the whole—alone no longer now
We will share the brightest parts of us, to create success—and how!

# SPRING

Spring was raising it's head today, life forces starting to flow
The sun came up, the mist was out, the sky was all aglow
A beautiful day unfolding with life, and refreshing us all anew
As the mist rolls away, both sky and sea, are reflecting in beautiful blue

All renewed, revived and enlivened—how fabulous our world feels
When the energy of the sun bursts forth, and everything old is healed
The mists cast eerie shapes and forms, around our Island shores
Ghostlike but very beautiful too, they just cannot be ignored

The nicest time of year, when daylight hours grow nice and long
And sunsets fill our night time skies, with such a colourful song
Blackness at last with a slice of bright moon, to light us on our way
And beautiful stars like diamonds shine—the end of a lovely day

## ANGER IN ME

Where is the anger, that lives deep inside
Where is it stored, and where does it hide
How is it accessed and brought to the fore
When I thought it wasn't inside me anymore
Hurtful and cruel, negative thoughts
All stemming from anger—is this the root cause

Tight knots in my stomach and pain in my chest
I just do not know, what to do for the best
'Out of Control'—is how my mind feels
When anger takes over from reason and steals . . .
Peace, calm and happiness, all torn away
Because anger took over my mind today

No warning or hint, of when it will come
Just a shocking reaction, to what someone's done
Frustration ensues, more feelings of rage
To be dealt with I know, but how can I engage
With this monster inside, that holds powers so huge
It controls my life, with it's own subterfuge

Eventual calm, at the end of the storm
But the damage means, everything's open and raw
Exhausted and spent, the monster retreats
Until it decides to run a repeat
I am working SO hard, I will tame this beast
Before it crushes me into it's final cruel feast

# REVENGE

There are many different aspects, to recovering from child abuse
At one point during healing, I felt so enraged I'd blow a fuse
Pure anger rose up inside me, oozing out into everyday life
Maybe I'd feel better if I had revenge on that man and his wife

My mind began to wander, creating scenarios of hate
I imagined things I could do to him—I just couldn't wait
Send a letter to all his neighbours—telling them what he'd done
But that would not help me, with my thoughts about my mum

Or I could burn their house down—sneaking up at dead of night
Sadly it was semi-detached, and I felt that it would not be right
For their kind neighbours to suffer, for the things that he had done
So I put that thought away, and then came up with another one

I could tamper with their car—hoping they would crash and burn
But the fact this could hurt someone else, gave me serious concern
I'd put an advert in the paper, and send it to everyone they knew
What could I really gain from this—I didn't have a clue

Finally I had to concede, that such cruel revenge would not be sweet
So I'd remove myself from their world—never again would we meet
Surely given time, they would regret and realise what they'd done
As me and mine removed ourselves—that was the day I knew I'd won

# A FANTASTIC DAY

A fantastic day sunny and clear—like my mind today
Positivity abounds, no space for fear—I can chase it away
Everything flows, like soft clouds in the sky
Simply being, and changing, and creating—no 'why'

'Why did this happen'—'Why did they do that'?
'I don't want to do this'—'Please can I go back'?
A mind full of purpose, and planning, and good
Has no space for 'How can I', 'I can't' or 'I should'

Just 'I am' and 'I have' and 'I can' and 'I do'
Then life and it's purpose, becomes clearer to you
Those words going round in your head every day
Need more censure and measure, than the words that you say

Negative quips—calling YOU names,
Or silly or stupid, or lacking in brains
'It's harmless' you say—'Just chatting away'
But repeated dozens of times every day???

You believe it you see—you decide 'this is me'
'I am worthy of nothing—no reason to be'
So in your head every day, just change what you say
And YOU too can create a truly Fantastic Day

# UNWORTHY

Who is it that is unworthy—it could be you or me
Something we feel in our hearts—so unreasonably
What makes us each decide, that somehow we are unfit
For something we wanted to do, it makes us want to quit

'Unworthy' is a difficult word—to try to understand
It seems to say we don't deserve, something we had planned
Then we think up lots of evidence, to confirm this silly thought
Compounding our disappointment, and leaving us distraught

Who told us we're unworthy—it happened many moons ago
We must have had it said to us, otherwise we couldn't know
It doesn't come up naturally, in everybody's life
Just when we're shown unkindness—sharp like a knife

It might have been our parent, who told us we were no good
At behaving well or helping them—we wouldn't have understood
Or siblings can be just as cruel, telling us how stupid we are
Another confirmation that we're no good, and we won't go far

So then these nasty little messages, burning like hot coals
Repeated over and over again, begin to destroy our souls
Our spirit lies in pieces, when this is all we're shown
I know this is the truth—for it's the only life I've known

## UNWORTHY Continued

Now I realise how foolish I'd be, to continue in this way
So I can tell myself I'm worthy—each and every day
I am not that small child now, so scared of everything
I challenge all those lies, and the trouble that they bring

I tell myself I CAN DO ANYTHING and I HAVE and I WILL
All positive messages—it feels like taking a happy pill!
The only voice I listen to, is the one that really cares
I've finally turned the tables, and now it's me who dares

So take a leaf from my book, understand how troubled they were
Those who made you feel unworthy—and now you must beware
And understand the choice is yours, to stop hearing their words
Allow your self-belief to soar—as high and free as the birds

When that little voice begins—negative affirmations in your head
Decide to change their meaning, into positives instead
Ensure that what you say to you, holds a message of pure love
You'll re-connect then with the universe—like a hand into a glove

# BELLS RING

An alarm clock is the first to ring, to wake us from our sleep
Once on the bus you ring the bell, to stop it on your street
Shop bells ring to warn of customers, waiting to be served
Mobiles go off in café's—ensuring everybody heard

Factories have their hooters, to set everything into motion
Schools also ring their morning bell—causing such commotion
Bells ringing on our microwave, toaster or such like
Sometimes appliances ring out, in the middle of the night

Sirens ring to warn us, of the ambulance speeding by
They have to get there quickly, or else someone may die
Police cars too have their own wail, must get out of their way
Be pleased they want to pass you by—not pull you over today

A fire truck with bells so loud, can be heard from far away
Dashing off and saving lives—still not getting enough pay
There's lots of car and property alarms—we hear them all the time
Just listening to them going off, we don't consider if there's a crime

Bells ring out from Big Ben, to mark each changing hour
With Sunday morning church bells all chiming in their tower
Wedding bells ringing out, announce celebrations can begin
Two people joining lives and then, cementing it with a RING!

# CHOICE

It really is your own choice—to feel happy or to feel sad
It took me quite a long time, to get my head round that!
I'd really always thought, other people affected how I felt
I didn't understand, it wasn't about, how my cards were dealt

I could decide to see the positive, in this life of mine
Stop focussing on anguish, and negativity all the time
'Everything happens for a reason'—a saying I believe is true
I won't pretend it's easy—what I'm asking you to do

Just know that it is so worthwhile—this is my gift to you
I confirm that choosing how to feel, is not something that's new
You can follow in my footsteps—I came out the other side
Together making progress, we can help others as their guide

# JUSTICE

I contemplated seeking justice, once I'd started to get help
Should I report my stepfather and would justice be dealt?
Initially I felt very strongly, that my own healing must come first
So I shelved this difficult question—it was one of the worst

After the shock of realisation, I found my anger forcing through
Making me reconsider justice, for this crime which was so taboo
My counsellor helped me to question, what this actually meant
I'd be raking it all up again and having to explain difficult content

What would I gain to go to court, against the man I'd called my Dad
He would not stand in front of me, and agree what he'd done was bad
It would always be my word against his, I had no proof of what he did
No one could make him admit, to something that our laws forbid

I agonised for many hours and hours, over what action I should take
The question I had to answer, was what did I want at the end of the day
Most of all I wanted to heal myself, from the sickness I'd carried so long
I knew if I could cleanse my mind, I would become someone very strong

My decision came very suddenly, I decided I would write to my Dad
I told him just what he had done, and what negative effects it had had
I never wanted to see him again, and I told him he must stay away
When I posted this momentous letter, for his signature I did pay

## JUSTICE Continued

So frightened once I'd sent it, but what could he do to me now
I realised I'd been in fear for so long, to release it I didn't know how
It took time for me to settle and realise there was nothing he could do
Finally my nightmare was over, now the people I cared about knew

My loved ones loved me as always, there had been no need to fear
I could concentrate on my healing, and know nothing could interfere
Divorced from my childhood family, I felt cleansed and free and true
And the justice I had craved, was something I'd internally pursue

That meant I would recover my life, begin again and learn who I am
Discovering things about me, my strengths and a new life programme
Starting with positive affirmations, I threw all negative messages out
My life would be truly valuable, my mental health way beyond doubt

I am happy to say I've achieved, more than I could ever have hoped
My loved ones are proud of me and impressed at the way I've coped
I love the life I am living, so complete now there is no doubt
My life is fulfilled and precious, and love has quenched my drought

# DEPRESSION

Hurting, crying—inside if not in sight
Waiting, hoping—for sense to come with the light
Night time lies heavy and dark in my heart
Pray for the morning and healing to start

Trying to be happy—keep smiling through the day
But spreading like ice, sadness chases it away
Barely coping now—each hour in a blur
Night time again, wonder what memories it will stir

Negative thoughts, ideas and fears filling up my head
It always happens this way, now I'm dreading going to bed
Wish I had a little switch, somewhere easy to locate
So I could get away, from this situation that I hate

Depression is so powerful and pushes you so low
It always takes you places, that you wouldn't choose to go
Old scenes and conversations, it manages to find
I didn't know that they, were even stored inside my mind

## DEPRESSION Continued

So many wounds left open—not gaping, just ajar
Enough to stop them healing, like a cut upon your arm
If you keep on pulling it open, as soon as it starts to heal
The pain can stay just out of sight, waiting to be revealed

They lie heavy in your body, all these little bits of pain
'Til their presence causes something, that you cannot contain
Will you have a nervous breakdown, or just a violent outburst
So before you take some tablets—please—let's look inside first

It takes some honest looking, and seeing with open eyes
To remove our own blinkers, and begin to self-analyse
I have triumphed in this battle—the battle for my own mind
Please know that you too have the power, to leave Depression behind

## AWAKE IN THE NIGHT

I'm laid awake again—more than two hours after coming to bed
Impossible to get to sleep, for the thoughts going round in my head
Keep considering the same questions, without any answers in sight
Strange how they converge upon me, in the middle of the night

Toss and turn, lie quite still—then just trying to relax
My brain continues regardless, considering all of the facts
It seems my mind has a mind of it's own, one I'm not privy to rule
I just can't remove my attention, as it continues to find it's own fuel

I don't understand how subjects unfold, unconnected as they can be
Asking 'why do I remember this?'—the only common thread is me
Memories dredged from years ago, or a new one from just last week
Does everybody experience this—or is it just me who's a freak

Sometimes it's a happy subject—and I realise I'm starting to smile
More often it's unpleasant, or boring—random items pulled from a file
Then imagined scenarios take over, in vivid visual form
These can be the worst of all, and can cause an emotional storm

Maybe it's something I've eaten, that's stopping me getting to sleep
Or is it because I was too hot, my covers are thrown off in a heap
Am I thirsty, or perhaps, just in need of the loo
Now I've tried everything—sleep is long overdue

I sneak out of the bedroom—mustn't wake my lovely man
I'll go and sit downstairs now, as I've come up with a plan
I will write down all this nonsense, for someone else to read
Then with my mind completely empty—sleep is guaranteed!

# THERAPY

I had to find a therapist, once my truth had been unleashed
Someone who would not judge me, but would help me find release
My counselling lady was so special, so kind and safe to me
Providing both an ear to hear, and a place I could just be

I poured out my resentment and anger—it lasted quite a long time
But my lady was so understanding, she informed me it was all benign
None of my memories could hurt me, not now in the cold light of day
And the magic her therapy offered, was to deal with it and send it away

Once she'd heard my explanation, of it's impact on my life
Her words contained suggestions, to cut through it like a knife
How did she understand so well and believe what I had said
Because she hadn't learned it . . . the same memories were in her head

Then I knew I'd found my helper, to start my journey home
I also knew I would win through—for now I was not alone
What that lady gave to me, mere words cannot describe
Suffice to say without her, I would not be alive

## FEAR

It seems that you are afraid of me—as I am afraid of you
And neither one of us, knows exactly what to do
To catch your eye and say hello, or simply walk on by
If we just ignore each other, we're both left wondering why

It starts way back when we start school, this socialising thing
We're told it's fun to go there, but alarm bells start to ring
Will we fit in? will they like us?—questions in our minds
Ensure that we're all ill at ease, all searching for the signs

It's all about the fear inside, that we won't be accepted
Infact, we all want the same thing: not to be rejected
Let's agree to treat each other, how we want to be treated too
That means that you'll be kind to me—and I'll be kind to you

# FORGIVENESS

Forgiveness—such a strange concept, I had always felt
I knew how to write the word—but just how was it dealt?
Pretending that you didn't mind, the awful thing someone had done
That seemed so ridiculous—and it would feel that they had won

I was told I must forgive them, that strange family of mine
'They hadn't known what they were doing and it had been such a long time'
'Forgive them and get over it, and then get on with my life'
That really felt impossible—the hurt was so sharp and alive

Then one day I understood—this concept of being able to forgive
It doesn't mean they did no wrong—or that they deserve to live
Dis-ease was created in me, by hatred for them that I nurtured inside
A poison not given to them, but swallowed by me each day of my life

Realisation hit—it was only me who hurt and felt sad
They had no comprehension, of the impact their actions had
So there really was no point, in just continuing to hate
Why would I want to hurt myself—a very damaging trait

There and then I decided to forgive, all that went before
I would forgive myself as well, and have peace forevermore
Now I just feel sorry, that they chose the life they did
And I know that forgiveness is necessary, for me to truly live

# GETTING HELP

I knew that now I'd started, I would have to see it through
I needed to find a Counsellor, there was so much work to do
I didn't feel that anyone else, could really know where to begin
So I found someone in the 'phone book, to help me go within

The lady was just amazing, so kind and calm and sure
She guided my investigations, into places so unpure
To say that it was difficult, is the understatement of the year
I found myself repeating words, I never thought I'd hear

I would leave our meetings sometimes, in a state of shock
At what she'd guided me to find, the doors she helped unlock
Tears would be streaming down my cheeks, all I could do was drive
Until I had calmed down enough, to go to work, where I could revive

My mind was so distracted, that my work suffered badly as well
I made some awful mistakes, but didn't have the courage to tell
Say what was happening to me? I just felt so totally ashamed
Felt I was fit for nothing—I should leave—I was to blame

## GETTING HELP continued

Looking back I don't know how I managed, to even go to work at all
It was so difficult to function, how I kept going I can't recall
It was as if there was a robot, who continued in my routine
All it managed to achieve, was to keep me fed and keep me clean

I wonder now what people thought, those who saw me every day
Inside I was crying out in pain, fighting a desperate need to run away
But I was so well practiced, in burying all my problems inside
That no-one was alerted, to the frightening place within my mind

You only need one person, who wants to help and believes in you
Then slowly progress can be made, as the hurt you begin to undo
Baby steps are needed, to rebuild the amazing person you should be
Just don't give up—I know it's hard—but you can win . . . like me

# UNKIND MIND

In the deep recesses of my mind
I find some things I left behind
Pain and sadness, hurt and fears
Accumulated through the years

Why does this happen again and again
Starting with tears and ending in pain
Can't find a solution to send it away
So I'm left to battle throughout the day

What is the trigger that opens this door
Then drags me inside, to dredge up some more
Unknown, unfelt—a huge storm unspent
I pray for relief—please let it all vent

One hour or two, a day or a few
Can drag into weeks—Do you feel like I do?
Can't stop the sadness, the terror, the pain
I seriously wonder, if I can stay sane

Consider the alternative—what could that be?
Sweet relief found in madness—a refuge for me
I hope it comes swiftly, I'm too tired to fight
So please take me there, before dark turns to light

## UNKIND MIND Continued

I find sleep at last, exhausted and spent
But dreams offer nothing, my mind won't relent
On waking I find, that I'm still in my mind . . .
It seems there's no way, that my mind can be kind

My whole body aches and my head's fit to burst
I cannot continue—have I been through the worst?
I need a solution, whatever the cost
I'm now realising, my battle is lost

Only one way to go—get out of this life
But do I have the courage—can I sacrifice ?
The hoping, wishing, striving to be the truly magnificent, wonderful me
That I know deep inside, I am meant to be

Now at rock-bottom, with few places to go
I choose to live life—now that I know . . .
I DO NOT WANT TO DIE—I WANT TO BE ME
I will deal with my mind, so that I can be free

# GRIEF

Grief is just so difficult, and painful to endure
Do we ever get over it? I'm not really sure
Personally my losses—though few and far between
Created pain inside me, that will be forever green

I've made a decision to say, that such feelings don't belong
For the deep and gripping sadness, just will not move along
I remember each occasion—so vivid in my mind
When a large and loving part of me, had to be left behind

Everyone just carries on—exactly as before
It's like nothing's happened, but my life's on the floor
I want to scream and shout out loud . . . but that's 'not what we do'
'Cos even in MY darkest hour I have to consider YOU

It would be so embarrassing, if I'd let my feelings show
And no-one would know what to do, they'd probably just go
It's not okay to sob and shake, when anyone's around
So I control myself, and manage not to make a sound

## GRIEF Continued

Then as the waves of sadness come, I choke the tears away
And pain spreads down into my chest, as I begin to sway
My legs just don't feel safe right now—I'd better find a chair
Mustn't make a show of myself, or people will start to stare

WHAT THE HELL IS WRONG WITH US WHEN SADNESS SHOWS IT'S FACE?
The way we're taught to deal with it—is an absolute disgrace
If I need to cry my heart out, then that's what I should do
Anything else is just a lie—whereas that would be my truth

I vow today to speak this message, to all my family and friends
To let them know what to expect—on this they can depend
I WILL NOT hold emotions in, when they plead to be set free
For finally I have learned, they serve a purpose within me

Permission is now given here, to everyone I know
To sob and cry and vent their pain—and truly let it go
Please understand the damage, that is stored within your heart
When you don't honour your loved one, from whom you have to part

# NO POINT

Before I discovered healing, I just felt there was no point
No point in living in this world, it seemed to always disappoint
The people who had brought me up, were not nurturing you see
So all of my childhood became, a battleground to me

Men and women all the same, none to choose between
Children, teens and adults, no-one honest and kind it seemed
I focussed on all the bad stuff—you know, it's always on TV
It compounded everything I thought—there was no reason to be

I could only see the beauty—very rarely—if at all
And the lovely feeling that gave me, very quickly began to pall
Laughter never lasted—beyond a moment or two
I couldn't find a connection, between me and someone like you

But once I discovered healing, truth and beauty were my goals
They both fed and rejuvenated me, with their contagious casserole
I felt I'd found what had been missing, in the time I'd spent on earth
I couldn't wait to devour it, my brain seemed to swell it was so alert

Now I feed my senses, and enjoy my life so much
I just don't have the words, to express this midas touch
Happiness abounds in my life, and I treasure everything that's there
I'll never be frightened again, of showing how much I care

Grateful is my middle name—I express it every day
I list the things I'm grateful for, so they can never slip away
Each morning I find something new—it's amazing how I can
And it starts with being grateful, to live with such an incredible man

## MOVING FORWARD

My counselling would only last, for a few very short weeks
Then I would be alone, so I would need a new technique
To continue healing by myself, and try to deal with the loss . . .
of my identity I felt, it seemed like such a double-cross

I had a really shocking thought: 'I do not know who I am'
shouted in my head, I felt my life had been a sham
It also meant I couldn't know, who I might have been
If my life had been normal and intelligence had intervened

But in this state, I couldn't decide—did I know me at all?
It was the weirdest feeling, was I heading for a fall
I had to close this train of thought, it disturbed me horribly
And I became afraid, of what I'd find when I found me

Eventually I realised, that I must start by loving me
My books were all insisting, self-love would set me free
It was very, very difficult to look myself in the eye
And say 'Janet I love you'—it hurt like I would die

I had never known that I, did not really love myself
I hadn't considered the concept—or even how it felt
So this would be the basis, of my recovery from all the pain
I'd have to look in my mirror, and repeat those words again

It took a very long time, until I believed what I said
But once I did I knew—I had an ally inside my head!
I never looked back to that lonely place, where I did not love me
I forgive myself and appreciate, that self-love has set me free

# HEALING

It happened one day, when a book came my way . . .
'You Can Heal Your Life' a book by Louise Hay
In our local library, it popped up in front of me
Very brightly coloured so it made me want to see
What lay inside such welcoming walls
I sat down to read and became enthralled

Louise was speaking directly to me with everything she had to say
How did she know? how could she see? it resonated straight away
So many of the things she'd written down
Were entrenched in my life and I was starting to drown
Not coping, not dealing—barely getting by
Life was so suffocating, I'd wanted to die

But now—Oh Wow!—I felt so alive
As I voraciously swallowed, the advice inside
This book so exciting, I couldn't believe
It should have 'SOLID GOLD' printed on its sleeve!
Fantastic! Just magic, my lifeline at last
It became my bible—it is unsurpassed

So I studied my book and worked very hard
To make changes to 'me,' where I'd been so scarred
As I learned new beliefs and challenged old ways
I created a 'new me' to continue my days
My essence is safe, I finally decide
With the wisdom and truth, I found deep inside

## HEALING Continued

Now I feel it's a pleasure to just be alive
Though I'm not pretending, that I 'have arrived'
I'm still learning and changing, and doing my best
To ensure that I'm able, to rise to the test
I'm now just beginning, to see why I'm here
I have much to offer, and I want to be clear

My life is to serve and help where I can
To offer some kindness, to my fellow man
If one person's pain, can be eased by my writings
Then my pen is the healer, and that's so exciting
It's so helpful to me, to write down my thoughts
When the pen with it's power, offers mutual support

So Louise—you have saved me—just one in the crowd
Your writings so powerful and their message so loud
I started my healing, by working with you
Now I know all the answers are inside me too
Please accept my thanks, from my soul to your own
For at last I can feel that I have come home

You'll continue your work, as I begin mine
My mentor, my saviour, my guide for all time
Healing together and with everyone else
The whole world is learning, to 'love the self'
Millions of people must thank you I know
So my words are their words: We All Love You So

# LOST

The things that are lost if you are abused, are many and diverse
You think of the obvious things that were lost, but some of the others are worse
I could have no trust in men now—they only think about one thing
I could have no trust in women too—they don't protect anything

Everything is about someone else and their selfishness inside
It only matters what THEY want—they will not apologise
Home is not a refuge, when your tormentors all live there
So nowhere can be safe and sound, there is no-one to care

If you are at the bottom of their pile, and left to cope alone
Then life hasn't any joy, inside this place you must call home
No love to be found to nurture, or warm you from inside
At best it offers you a place, that you can use to hide

For how scary must the world be, if this is your safest place of all
You dare not venture outside, for it seems guaranteed you'll fall
So life becomes a place of fear—that's what it always was to me
There could be nothing good there, so I really didn't want to see

# LOST Continued

'I lived my whole life long in fear'—is a line from a poem of mine
It is so true—I cannot stress the importance of his crime
It took away everything good, and replaced it all with fear
It's an absolute miracle of life, that I'm even standing here

Now I'm rebuilding my 'life reference', and I have a man of love
I also have an amazing daughter, who was sent from up above
My home is filled with laughter and love, and all things that are good
The fear has been expelled at last, now that I've understood

That nothing had been taken, from my sweet and beautiful life
I am so happy now, just to be my amazing husband's wife
Everything good was waiting, out of sight but safe and sound
Until my mind convinced me, that my essence had been found

I am a new found person—one I recognise, it's true
And one that probably looks the same, to everyone I knew
But inside the transformation, illuminates my exquisite soul
And now life is complete for me—everything is Pure Gold

# DISTRACTIONS

Once you start to change your behaviour, and experience a new way to be
You will see that you are in charge of your life, as well as your own sanity
Perhaps you're addicted to sadness—just used to feeling down
Or maybe you're a stress junkie—so life means dashing around

Perhaps if you aren't worrying—you feel that you don't care?
Or if you aren't overworked—does that make you despair?
Sometimes we use these methods, to keep our minds from looking in
To try and find what matters inside, would feel like such a sin

Maybe never accepting silence—does this one sound like you?
Noise is the final hiding place, it divides your soul in two
Distractions come in many forms, we are experts in this field
Maintaining disjointed thought patterns, prevents us being healed

Silence is just so pure—it will allow you to really hear
Your inner voice which guides you, it's message true and clear
Spend time away from background noise, it holds you in a dream
TV, radio, computer talk—just like a moth around a light beam

Release yourself—release your mind—just try it for a while
And begin to get to know yourself—you'll find you start to smile
Free your thoughts from stimulus, and allow them peace to be
Some quiet time will calm your world and make you happier—you'll see

# WORDS

Words are just amazing and can be used for so many things
Creative strings of letters—what pleasure these can bring
Words moulded into stories, to while the hours away
Probably how it all started, back in our ancestors' day

We must memorise our alphabet, and learn to write it down
First practicing our letters, then learning verbs and nouns
Dream up a simple story, one to entertain our friends
'Exciting' to begin with and probably 'Happy' at the end!

Books to read, subjects galore—not reading just for fun
But studying now to learn a skill, probably more than one
Then getting into novels, intrigue buried in their plots
Keep us engrossed, and occupied, joining up the dots

Real life can be translated, with language colourful and raw
In newspapers and magazines, articles cutting to the core
There's rhyming words, poetry and prose, all fighting to be heard
No matter what the subject—usually leaving emotions stirred

Lists are just superb to read—we make them all the time
I check the list inside my head, to find a word that rhymes
Signs and instruction leaflets, to explain what we must do
And all the dreaded 'small print', created to confuse me and you

We'll have to write our notice, to leave our job, a flat or such
Whilst letters to friends and family, help us all keep in touch
Words spoken when we're living—some spoken over us when we die
We cannot live without words—now I'll have to write down why!

# JUDGING

Why do we want to judge someone—is it what we're all taught to do?
So when we look out from our world, automatically some judgement is due
On whom we decide to cast judgement, is not so easily defined
Often we select our targets, when they mirror some part of our mind

So let us consider together, what this judging really means
Does projected negativity, prevent our faults from being seen?
Must we criticize each other, to make us feel better inside
And avoid the bad thoughts about us, that we nurture in our minds

We might judge random people, as we pass by them in the street
And judging one of our peers, can make us somewhat less discreet
Comments we feel justified, about someone we do not know
Become vitriolic diatribes, about one of those closer to home

We believe that all attention, is drawn away from ourselves
Whilst we're ranting and complaining, about somebody else
Highlighting all of their faults, means that you won't see our own
Actually it just confirms, how petty minded we have grown

## JUDGING Continued

So if I'm pointing out someone's faults, when they are an absentee
It's mainly just to distract you, from focussing attention on me
Doesn't it sound pathetic—once we hear it all explained
But this is how we function, and we are all to be blamed

For myself I've decided to try, with my heart and soul, I swear
To stop my need for judgement, and instead show that I care
Whether to a stranger, as I pass by them in the street
Or my peers, friends and neighbours—infact everyone I meet

'One day at a time'—that's how the saying goes
I try now just to listen, and stop thinking that I know
And slowly I will change, these really unacceptable ways
To become a better person, who is rid of that negative haze

Do you question why we do this—or even acknowledge that you do?
Whatever explanation you're thinking of, please consider it's untrue
It's such an unhealthy pastime, eating away at your soul
I beg you to reconsider, and make loving acceptance your goal

# GRATITUDE

I am grateful just to be alive!—never thought I would say that
But achieving some self-healing, has put me back on my life path
It isn't clear what holds us back—but in my case it was me
Now I'm living life at last, and learning how I can 'just be'

Gratitude is a small word—for what I actually feel
I'm not sure how to say it, except it makes me want to kneel
To offer thanks and gratitude, to every living thing
As we are all connected—it makes my spirit sing

So focus on what you're grateful for—it's easy if you try
It just changes life's perspective, so good feelings amplify
It's your choice to stay in negative mode—a habit too I fear
But if you would try the opposite, your pathway will be clear

'What have I to be grateful for?'—your thoughts start to jeer
Then basic things that mean the most, are whispered in your ear
Maybe living in a very safe place, could be top of your list
Then nature and all it's beauty, are definitely not to be missed

A friend you can rely on; good food to eat each day;
The funds to take a holiday when you need to get away;
Some family and pets; maybe a partner by your side
All the special and important things, that brighten up our lives

# PAINTING

At school I didn't seem, to have an artistic side
And whatever I created, I'd always try to hide
The obligatory lessons, throughout my childhood years
Did nothing to encourage me, they just confirmed my fears

I was never going to create, an inspired piece of art
So no need for me to take, my teacher's criticism to heart
I haven't tried to draw or paint, since those uninspired days
Until a painting friend suggested, that it could be fun to play

It took more than a couple of years, until I finally succumbed
And what she helped me to produce, left me completely stunned
Such an amazing feeling—messing around with paint
And now she'd got me so intrigued, to see what I'd create

We spent many hours together, as she taught me what to do
And convinced me that if I just tried, I truly would win through
She helped me to make pictures, that are really rather nice
Infact she's taught me something, that has really changed my life

It's like a meditation, I get so engrossed you see
And what I am creating, is inspired inside me
I have taken a good lesson, from this experience with my friend
And my usual 'I can't' attitude—I've started to amend

# THE NEW ME

Now I need to tell everybody, just exactly how my life has changed
It started with learning to 'love myself'—this concept frazzled my brain!
I also stopped completely, the internal chatter that criticised me
This was so incredibly liberating—it was me setting myself free!

With these two important changes, where I felt I was winning through
I tackled the problem of healing—it seemed such a massive task to do
I learned that I did have intelligence and was able to think for myself
This opened up a fantastic arena, for me to improve my own health

Please know: I write of my mental health, as well as the physical side
Realising emotional trauma, had caused dis-ease in my body and mind
I was certain I could find freedom, from the old and well-trodden path
My emotional health would support me, as I dealt with the aftermath

Changing negative thoughts I'd clung on to—believing them correct
Proved such a powerful process, it had a hugely uplifting effect
Where I'd said No I said Yes; I Can't became I Can and I Will!
All things I'd never done before, I really put myself through the mill

## THE NEW ME Continued

This gave me some confidence, which previously did not exist
Enabling me to reach further and experience key things from my list
What I did is not important, for my goals will be different to yours
What matters is though I was terrified, instinct told me I was on course

To recap I'll just confirm to you, I was 43 years old when I realized
What had happened to almost destroy me, throughout my early life
For another 10 years I floundered, trapped in my 'wilderness years'
At 53 I began my healing journey, and finally to deal with the fear

Now I feel like a child is reborn, inside this precious body of mine
I can see all the beauty around me, as well as that inside my mind
I'm just deeply grateful to be alive and can't find words to explain
I enveloped the child within me, and began to dissolve all her pain

For me life could not be better—though it still improves each day!
I have everything I could wish for and just love everything I survey
So please: don't give in to your sadness—you too can feel as I do
Be grateful each day to be alive and our universe will support you